Communication & Popular Culture Coursebook

Third Edition

Colorado State University

Nick Marx
Mark Saunders

Kendall Hunt
publishing company

Cover image © Shutterstock, Inc.

Kendall Hunt
publishing company

www.kendallhunt.com
Send all inquiries to:
4050 Westmark Drive
Dubuque, IA 52004-1840

Copyright © 2013, 2014, 2018 by Kendall Hunt Publishing Company

ISBN 978-1-5249-5512-0

Published in the United States of America

CONTENTS

Unit 1: Popular Culture Texts

Unit 2: Popular Culture Industries

Unit 3: Popular Culture & Historical Context

Unit 4: Popular Culture Audiences & Technologies

COURSE DESCRIPTION

What is popular culture? How does popular culture communicate with us through media? Out of what historical, commercial, and creative contexts does American popular culture emerge? These broad questions fuel our work in this course. **Communication & Popular Culture** presents an introduction to U.S. popular culture, with an emphasis on its forms and functions in our society. First, we engage with four key domains that construct popular culture's meanings in order to empower students with the critical skills to understand cultural texts. Second, we consider how popular culture has both shaped and reflected broader social power dynamics in the United States. Finally, we analyze popular culture in detailed written arguments and cogent oral presentations. Because this is an All-University Core Curriculum course, we have specific objectives: to place the history of popular culture within a broader context of U.S. history; to analyze a variety of texts that loosely fall into the category "arts and humanities," and to suggest particular methods of critical thinking.

COURSE OBJECTIVES

- To describe the popular culture texts from a Communication Studies perspective and to define and utilize key media analysis terms.
- To explain the relationship between popular culture texts and their socio-historical contexts.
- To analyze the industries that produce popular culture texts.
- To analyze the power of popular culture texts to represent and shape social power and cultural identities.
- To critique and construct arguments about popular culture and/as communication through research, writing, and civic or cultural engagement.

OVERVIEW OF ASSIGNMENTS

Accountability/Assessments: 100
- *May include in-class and/or online quizzes, exams and reflections on assigned readings, videos, and lecture materials.*

Participation = 50
- *May include in-class activities, impromptu reflections, or other tasks based on the instructor's discretion.*

Illustrated Glossary = 100
- *Define a given pop cultural textual analysis term, find an appropriate or relevant illustration of a given pop cultural textual analysis term, and then explain how your example represents that term.*

Narrative Group Method lab = 100
- *Identify and explain the various aesthetic and narrative components of a given pop culture text.*

Pop Culture Pitch = 100
- *Research and synthesize main ideas from primary documents for a given culture industry text, trend, or practice. Research and describe the current climate of culture industries. Describe the ideological implications of culture as a commercial enterprise.*

Historical Context Individual Method Lab = 150
- *Identify and describe the key socio-historical contexts out of which your pop culture text emerges.*

Annotated Bibliography = 100
- *Find and analyze secondary scholarly sources that support a research question. Cite a source in APA or MLA format. Summarize and assess a scholarly source. Utilize a scholarly source as evidence in support of an argument.*

Final Essay = 200

- *Argue persuasively about the meaning of a pop cultural text. Research and synthesize evidence from the industrial, historical, and textual domains of their chosen topic and explain how they interact in support of the text's meaning.*

Final Exam: Museum Exhibit Poster = 100

- *Visually represent an historical pop culture case study through pictures and research. Describe the relationship between the histories of race, gender, or sexuality in the United States and their role in pop culture texts.*

TOTAL = 1000 points

FINAL GRADE SCALE

967 − 1000 = A+	867 − 899 = B+	767 − 799 = C+	600 − 699 = D
933 − 966 = A	833 − 866 = B	700 − 766 = C	0 − 599 = F
900 − 932 = A−	800 − 832 = B−		

Students will be evaluated in accordance with University grading policy & guidelines. In calculating final grades, consideration will be focused in such areas as the ability to understand and discuss fundamental course concepts, the ability to work both independently and collaboratively (in class discussions, activities, and out-of-class work), and the successful application of critical skills.

COURSE POLICIES

Notes on Attendance and Participation

Although no attendance will be taken during lectures, **attendance is essential for success in the course.** <u>You must be present for the entire class period in order to get credit for any in-class and/or group activities.</u> In the event you miss a lecture, you are nevertheless responsible for all material discussed in that class. Copies of lectures will only be distributed to students with either a University-sanctioned excuse or documented medical or family emergency situation. In this case, it is still your responsibility to meet with the instructor to go over any information missed. Furthermore, it is recommended that you also supplement this information with another student's notes. Effective and consistent participation can also improve your final grade in cases where your numerical grade is on the cusp between final letter grades. Participation can be achieved by answering questions in class (and in doing so, respecting the ideas of fellow students) and seeing the instructor during office hours.

Accommodations

CSU provides many resources for temporarily and permanently disabled students through the office for Resourses for Disabled Students. They can be contacted as follows:

General Services Building 100 / http://rds.colostate.edu/ / (970) 491-6385 (V/TDD)

Also, please see me to discuss any learning or access issues at your convenience.

Academic Integrity / Student Conduct Code / Honor Pledge

This course adheres to the Academic Integrity Policy of the Colorado State University General Catalog and the Student Conduct Code (http://www.conflictresolution.colostate.edu/conduct-code#conduct) and will be utilizing the recently approved "Honor Pledge" (http://tilt.colostate.edu/integrity/honorpledge/index.cfm) for all assignments. A key feature of academic integrity is avoiding plagiarism. It is important to understand how the University defines plagiarism: "**the copying of language, structure, ideas, or thoughts of another, and**

representing them as one's own without proper acknowledgment. Examples include a submission of purchased research papers as one's own work; paraphrasing and/or quoting material without properly documenting the source." (CSU General Catalog: http://catalog.colostate.edu/front/policies.aspx). All written assignments must be your own, and must be original and specific to this course. **Work originally written for another course is *not* acceptable**. Material taken from other sources **must be appropriately cited**. Links on the Canvas site and other course materials describe proper citation procedures. We will discuss ways to avoid plagiarism, and I am happy to discuss research techniques with you if you have questions. **Plagiarism degrades your intelligence**. If you are found to have plagiarized any of your work in this course, you may be liable for disciplinary action as discussed in the CSU General Catalog and Student Conduct Code (see links on Canvas to these documents).

Vericite

The Department of Communication Studies employs Vericite to protect against plagiarism, and it is MANDATORY that you submit your Final Essay to the service. Vericite can be accessed through your class's Canvas site, and because it is linked to Canvas, you do not have to register separately. After clicking on the appropriate assignment, you can upload your paper in a variety of formats (although Word documents tend to work most smoothly). **Be sure to confirm that you successfully submitted your assignment by re-clicking on the Vericite link after you've submitted** (you can then see if your assignment is being processed). Your instructor may enable Vericite to allow you to submit a working draft and see a report. If this is the case, you will see a separate entry for this option under Assignments. This draft will NOT be graded and submission is optional. You may change any or all of your work after receiving a report. In any case, you MUST submit a final version of your assignment.

A Note About Content

Some of the material screened in class may feature graphic violence, language, and/or sexuality, and may be offensive to some students. Please contact me if you feel the course content is too objectionable, and alternate screenings may be assigned.

Technology in the Classroom

Please silence your phone and refrain from messaging during class (especially during screenings). If you must message, please leave the room to do so. All laptops must be turned off during screenings as well.

Instructor Responsibilities

- Be prepared for lecture, and available for explanation and assistance outside of class if requested.
- Treat all students with courtesy and respect.
- Be open to constructive input from students in the course.
- Ensure that opportunities to participate are enjoyed equally by all students in the course.
- Efficiency, consistency, and fairness in grading.

Student Responsibilities

- Come to class on time, and refrain from packing up belongings before class ends.
- Keep up with the reading and fulfill assignments as scheduled.
- Turn off all electronic devices that might create a disruption in class.
- When speaking, use courteous, respectful language.
- Ask questions of course materials, the instructor, and yourself.
- Ask for help when you need it.

SPCM100 COURSE CONTRACT

This class can be **<u>awesome</u>**. Students tend to really enjoy this course and get a lot out of it. If you follow directions, come to every class, pay attention, and put in time and effort, you will most likely do well and learn a lot about a very relevant subject. If you don't, you won't. Let's work together to have a great semester.

I, [print name] _____, have read over the Course Syllabus, Course Description, Objectives, Assignments, and Policies and now understand them. By signing this, I am rejecting my right to say, "I didn't read that!", "I wasn't aware of that policy," "I didn't know that was due today," "I didn't know that was going to be required," "Uhhh, I didn't, like, know that, like, totally," etc.

_____   _____

Signature   Date

Section Number: SPCM100-_____

SPCM100 HONOR PLEDGE

I will not give, receive, or use any unauthorized assistance when completing the assignments for this course.

_____   _____

Signature   Date

Section Number: SPCM100-_____

ASSIGNMENT GRADING SCALES

200 Point Scale

A+:   193.5 – 200
A: 187 – 193
A–:   180 – 186.5
B+:   173.5 – 179.5
B: 167 – 173
B–:   160 – 166.5
C+:   153.5 – 159.5
C: 140 – 153
D: 120 – 139.5
F: 0 – 119.5

100 Point Scale

A+:   97 – 100
A: 93.5 – 96.5
A–:   90 – 93
B+:   87 – 89.5
B: 83.5 – 86.5
B–:   80 – 83
C+:   77 – 79.5
C: 70 – 76.5
D: 60 – 69.5
F: 0 – 59.5

150 Point Scale

A+:   145 – 150
A: 140 – 144.5
A–:   135 – 139.5
B+:   130 – 134.5
B: 125 – 129.5
B–:   120 – 124.5
C+:   115 – 119.5
C: 105 – 114.5
D: 90 – 104.5
F: 0 – 89.5

50 Point Scale

A+:   48.5 – 50
A: 47 – 48
A–:   45 – 46.5
B+:   43.5 – 44.5
B: 42 – 43
B–:   40 – 41.5
C+:   38.5 – 39.5
C: 35 – 38
D: 30 – 34.5
F: 0 – 29.5

PAPER GRADING CRITERIA

"A" (**"Exemplary"**) **Paper:** Follows all of the formatting guidelines; an exceptionally well-written paper with no typos or errors in grammar, spelling, and punctuation; superior fluency and readability; combines thoughtful opinion, specific examples, and clear analysis; goes beyond summary and offers well-argued interpretations; appropriate depth; is accurate with answers, opinions, textual facts, and application of class concepts.

"B" (**"Proficient"**) **Paper:** Follows most of the formatting guidelines; some typos and/or occasional errors in grammar, spelling, or punctuation; good fluency with some sentences that need revision; includes some opinion, examples, and analysis; mixes summary and interpretation; responds with some depth; mixes up only a few or minor details with textual facts or class concepts.

"C" (**"Developing"**) **Paper:** Formatting guidelines inconsistently followed; contains frequent typos and/or consistent errors in grammar, spelling, and punctuation; does not demonstrate a clear understanding of the text or does not include much opinion, examples, and analysis; has more summary than interpretation; responds with little depth; may not meet minimum length requirement; several or notable inaccuracies with textual facts and/or application of class concepts.

"D" (**"Beginning"**) **Paper:** Extensive formatting issues; multiple typos and grammar, spelling and punctuation problems; does not respond with any depth; does not include any opinion, examples, or analysis; is mostly all summary with no interpretation; does not meet minimum length requirement; the analysis is wrong; is not accurate with textual facts and application of class concepts.

TIPS FOR WRITING SPCM100 PAPERS

- Take the time to punctuate sentences, quotes, and text titles properly (please consult a style manual and be consistent). Also, you can refer to the Punctuating Titles Guidelines in the Coursebook. For example, music album titles are either underlined or italicized, but song titles go in quotation marks. Thus, an example from a paper might sound like this: I chose to analyze the song "Come Together" from the Beatles' album *Abbey Road*.

- Be sure to connect quotes to your own words by leading into them, or following up behind them. An example from a paper might sound like this: As Caroline Smith stated in an article from *Newsweek,* "Pop culture trends are constantly changing" (34). Another example could be: "That musician is completely over-rated," stated one recent critic in regards to the singer's last album (Ramirez 12).

- Do not put empty lines between paragraphs in your papers. They are not needed and waste space. Also, be sure you're using the proper text size, style, and margin width. Instructors can tell when students adjust those to make it look like they've written more or less to meet the page requirements.

- Use the spell check function on your computer, but also proofread your papers. Even have family members and friends who have a strong grasp of writing skills edit your papers, as well. It's worth it! Plus, all CSU students have access to the free Writing Center located in the basement of Eddy Hall, Room 23. Consultants will edit papers for content, not proofread for spelling, grammar, punctuation errors, though. Consultations are available both in person and online; more information can be found on their website (http://writing-center.colostate.edu/).

- When citing sources, you need to include both in-text citations (actually in the text of the paper) and formal citations on the Works Cited page. Be sure to follow the proper format for each type of citation and the proper indentation style for the page. For example, if an in-text citation includes a title, then the title must be punctuated properly. Also, when using MLA format, the page where you list your citations should be titled Works Cited. The page title does not need to go in quotes or be underlined/italicized, etc. See the example on the next page and a style manual for more details.

- A general guideline is that whatever information is listed first in a citation on the Works Cited page is what goes in the **in-text (parenthetical)** citation in the paper. This is usually the author's last name for MLA. Avoid including web addresses (like, www.printmedia.com). Instead, state the author's last name or the title of the twitter/blog post or web article/entry (not the web address or website!) if the author's name is not available. An MLA example for citing a web article that didn't have an author might be: According to one on-line article, this movie was a "complete bomb" ("Movie Disasters from 2009"). **Web addresses are required on the Works Cited page for this course.**

For help with MLA in-text source citations and the Works Cited Page, go to:

http://www.library.cornell.edu/resrch/citmanage/mla

http://owl.english.purdue.edu/owl/resource/747/01/

Example MLA Works Cited Page:

Works Cited

Dobbin, Ben. "Male-Studies—Not Just a Guy Thing." *Los Angeles Times,* 20 July 1997: E1, E4.

Garner, Dwight. "Sissyhood is Powerful: Man's Journey from Iron John to Ironing Johns." *Salon Magazine* 7, 10 Feb. 1996. 18 Oct. 2009. <http://www.salonmagazine.com/07/reviews/ manhood.html>.

"Mr. and Mrs. Smith (2005)." *Imdb.com.* 18 Oct. 2009. <http://www.imdb.com/title/tt0356910/>.

PUNCTUATING TITLES GUIDELINES

*A general guideline is that titles for major/primary works (music album, television series, etc.) go in italics or are underlined, while specific parts of works (songs, television episodes, etc.) go in quotation marks.

Titles and Names That Should Be Italicized (or Underlined)

Note: choose either to italicize or to underline these types of titles in your papers (do not mix the two!).

- Album (e.g., Taylor Swift's *1989*)
- Book
- Comic/Cartoon
- Drawing
- Encyclopedia
- Film
- Magazine
- Newspaper
- Painting
- Pamphlet
- Play
- Sculpture or statue
- Television series (e.g., *Stranger Things*)

Titles That Should Go in Quotation Marks

- Article in a newspaper or magazine (whether in print or digital)
- Commercial
- Individual episode in a television series (like "Fifteen Percent," an episode of *Modern Family)*
- Poem
- Short story
- Skit / sketch / routine
- Song

Exceptions to the Rules / Extra Tips

- Religious works are not underlined or italicized (e.g., The Bible or The Torah)
- Building and monuments are not given extra punctuation (e.g., The Washington Monument)

UNIT 1: POPULAR CULTURE TEXTS

What is a popular culture "text," and what does it mean to analyze one? As Jonathan Gray notes:

> A text is a unit of meaning for interpretation and understanding. As such, most things are (or could be treated as) texts. Within media studies, a text could be a television program, film, video game, website, book, song, podcast, newspaper article, tweet, or app. Texts matter because they are bearers of communication and movers of meaning. Texts can inspire and delight, or disgust and disappoint, but more importantly they intervene in the world and into culture, introducing new ideas, or variously attacking or reinforcing old ones. Textual analysis has long been a primary mode of "doing" media studies, as scholars seek to ascertain what a text means, *how* it means (what techniques are used to convey meaning), and what its themes, messages, and explicit and implicit assumptions aim to accomplish.[1]

Because texts are often our initial encounter with popular culture's complex meanings, the first unit for this course begins by having students look at terms and concepts for describing what we hear and see onscreen. Next, it helps students understand how the visual cues of pop culture texts build more complex ideas through narrative patterns. Finally, it asks students to consider how and why popular culture texts are part of broader systems of signification, ones whose commercial motivations we'll examine more closely in Unit 2: Popular Culture Industries.

[1]Gray, Jonathan, "Text." in Laurie Ouellette and Jonathan Gray (eds), *Keywords for Media Studies.*New York: NYU Press, 2017, 196.

UNIT 1: POPULAR CULTURE TEXTS: ILLUSTRATED GLOSSARY (100 POINTS)

Objectives:

- To describe the popular culture texts from a Communication Studies perspective and to define and utilize media analysis terms.
- To analyze the power of popular culture texts to represent and shape social power and cultural identities.

Student Learning Outcomes:

Students will be able to

- Find an appropriate or relevant illustration of a given pop cultural textual analysis term.
- Explain how your example represents that term.

Description: In this assignment, you will define a list of textual analysis terms. For each of the terms you will provide a **definition of the term, a visual example of the term—a frame grab or still from a movie or television show—**and a **written explanation** of how the visual example highlights that term. You may use the frame grab/still more than once. The frame grab/still does not have to come from a movie or television show, but typically it will. You do not have to cite the frame grab/still. You do not need a works cited page for the pictures. Since your written explanation will be in your own words, you do not need to cite that either.

Terms

Mise En Scene	Extreme close up	Deep focus	Eye level angle
Close up	Shallow focus	Secondary prominence	Dominant prominence
Low angle	Long shot	High contrast lighting	High key lighting
Low key lighting	High angle	Mechanical/practical special effects	Digital special effects
Extreme long shot		Medium shot	

GRADING RUBRIC—UNIT 1: ILLUSTRATED GLOSSARY

	Exemplary	Proficient	Developing	Beginning
Quality **80 points**	Written explanations demonstrate a clear and thorough understanding of how illustrations represent terms, relevant to pop culture texts. (80–72 points)	Most written explanations demonstrate a clear and thorough understanding of how illustrations represent terms. (71–64 points)	Some written explanations demonstrate a clear and thorough understanding of how illustrations represent terms – some writing is short, rushed, or not relevant to pop culture texts. (63–56 points)	Few written explanations demonstrate a clear and thorough understanding of how illustrations represent terms—writing is short, rushed, or not relevant to pop culture texts. (55–0 points)
Mechanics **20 points**	Few to no distracting errors in spelling, grammar, or mechanics. (20–18 points)	Some distracting errors in spelling, grammar, or mechanics. (17–16 points)	Several distracting errors in spelling, grammar, or mechanics. (15–14 points)	Too many distracting errors to be considered a final draft. (13–0 points)

Points: _____ / 100

ILLUSTRATED GLOSSARY: TERMS & DEFINITIONS

Mise En Scene: Placing on a stage. Or putting into the scene. It can be spontaneous or planned. Mise en Scene is useful for analyzing any popular culture text: a scene in a film, a television show, advertisements, commercials, photographs, art work, or music videos.

SHOTS

EXTREME LONG SHOT: Used to demonstrate scale (often an **Establishing Shot**)
ESTABLISHING SHOT: Sets the scene where the action takes place.
LONG SHOT: Entire human figure visible – top of head to bottom of feet.
MEDIUM SHOT: Near the waist – torso & head. There can have variable degrees (**Medium-Long** and **Medium-Close Up**).
CLOSE- UP SHOT: Head (& Shoulders) only.
EXTREME CLOSE-UP SHOT: Specific part of the face.
POV SHOT: (Point of View) From the subject's perspective (eyes).

ANGLES

LOW ANGLE: Looking up at subject. Camera is positioned low on vertical axis. Subject has *power*.
HIGH ANGLE: Looking down at subject. Camera is positioned high on vertical axis. Subject is *weak*.
EYE LEVEL: Looking directly at subject. *Empathy* and *equality* with subject.
BIRD'S EYE: "God view" looking directly down. *Smallness* or *insignificance* of subject.

FOCUS

SHALLOW: One plane is in focus. It forces the viewer to look there.
DEEP: Everything is in focus. For the viewer everything is available to look at.

Dominant: What is our eye attracted to first (usually friendly faces)?
Secondary: Where does the eye go after the dominant?

LIGHTING

HIGH KEY: Bright, well lit. Comedy and romance.
LOW KEY: Dark. Mystery and horror.
CONTRAST: Difference between dark and light.

Special effects: Mechanical, optical, or digital illusions within the text.

ILLUSTRATED GLOSSARY:
ADDITIONAL TERMS (FOR YOUR REFERENCE)

CUTS

JUMP CUTS: Abrupt transition in time and/or space that calls attention to itself.

MATCH CUTS: Cut of two different compositions in which objects in the two shots graphically match, often helping to establish a strong continuity of action and linking the two shots metaphorically. Can also be called a graphic match.

MATCH-ON-ACTION: Activity is continued from one shot to next

EYELINE MATCH: Character is looking in a direction that is motivated by narrative

SHOT-COUNTER SHOT / REVERSE ANGLE: Character **A** is looking at another character (often off screen). Then, Character **B** is shown looking back at Character **A**. Characters are shown facing opposite directions. Viewer assumes they are facing each other. Follows the 180 Degree rule.

REACTION: Facial expression of person who is not talking in a scene is removed

CROSS CUT: One scene comments on another

CUT AWAY: A shot that's usually of something other than the current action. It could be a different subject (a cat when the main subject is its owner), a close up of a different part of the subject (the subject's hands), or just about anything else. Adds interest and information.

FRAMING & SYMMETRY

TIGHT: Characters don't have room to move around within the shot. Can connote constraint.

LOOSE: Characters have plenty of room to move around within the shot. Can connote freedom.

VERTICAL: Items within the shot create vertical lines. Can connote height, power, or imprisonment.

HORIZONTAL: Items within the shot create horizontal lines. Can connote length, magnitude, or openness.

DIAGONAL: Items within the shot create diagonal lines. Can connote movement or disorientation.

RULE OF THIRDS: the frame is divided into nine imaginary sections. This creates reference points which act as guides for framing the image. (Picture at right)

EMPTY SPACES: Uncentered framing of the subject. Connotes loneliness or that something is missing.

CAMERA MOVEMENT

PAN: Pointing the camera *horizontally*, left and right, with respect to the subject.

WHIP PAN: A pan shot in which the camera moves sideways so quickly that the picture blurs into indistinct streaks. Commonly used as a transition, and can indicate the passage of time and/or a frenetic pace of action.

TILT: **Pointing** the camera *vertically*, up and down, (as opposed to moving the whole camera up and down). Changes angle, not position.

PED: (Pedestal) Moving the camera **position** *vertically,* up and down, with respect to the subject.

FOLLOW: The camera physically follows the subject at a more or less constant distance.

TRACKING, TRUCKING, or DOLLY: The camera is mounted on a cart which travels along tracks for a very smooth movement.

ZOOM: Change in the lens focal length with gives the illusion of moving the camera closer or further away. Not technically a camera movement.

STEADICAM: A stabilizing mount which mechanically isolates the operator's movement from the camera, allowing a very smooth shot.

HANDHELD ("Shaky cam" or "shaky" or "unstable"): Stable-image techniques are dispensed with on purpose. The camera is handheld, or given the appearance of being handheld. Shaky cam gives a film sequence a documentary film feel. It suggests unprepared, unrehearsed filming of reality.

TRANSITIONS

FADE-OUT: Darkens image until black.

FADE-IN: Starts black and then illuminates.

FADES: Together, they mark a substantial change in *time*.

DISSOLVE: 1st shot fades out while next shot fads in. Overlap. Passage of *time*. Slow dissolve = more time.

WIPE: One image wipes another off the screen (think of a windshield wiper). Change in *space* (or time).

BLUR: Dream sequence.

SOUND BRIDGE: Audio / video is staggered. Next scene's audio is heard before the visual cut. Music tying together separate scenes (montages).

PACE

SLOW: One plot line: 1950s television.

STEADY: One or two plot lines, few characters: *All in the Family, The Cosby Show.*

RAPID: Multiple plot lines, quick transitions, non-sequiturs: *30 Rock, How I Met Your Mother, The Family Guy, 24.*

FRENETIC: Music Videos.

SETS

4TH WALL: Set is open to audience and cameras where the fourth wall should be. Ex: *Friends*

CLOSED: Set is closed on all sides to look real. Ex: *House*

ON LOCATION: No set. Filming is done at a real-life local. Ex: *Friday Night Lights*

SOUND

VOCAL SOUNDS: Talk, whisper, yell, echo.

DIALOGUE:
- TONE: Pessimistic, serious, humor, depressed, playful, suspicious, lighthearted, dark, angry, ironic, sarcastic, cheerful, afraid, sad, matter-of-fact, whimsical, gloomy, fun, nostalgic, sorrowful, sarcastic, romantic...
- RATE: Slow, Steady, Rapid, Frenetic (see above in "Pace").

MUSIC:
- SCORE: Tone (see above in "Dialogue").
- LICENSED MUSIC: mood
  o MOODS: Tense, light, frustration, gloomy, happiness, sorrow, romance, sentimental, suspense, sadness, suspicion, fear, paranoia, nostalgia, whimsy, serious, pain, etc.
- THEME SONG: Underlines essence of the show.

ENVIRONMENTAL SOUNDS: Within the show.

- AMBIENT: Primary sound sources (created in the show environment) – footsteps, voices.
- SOUND EFFECTS: Secondary sound sources (added later) – roars, punches, doorbells.

DIEGETIC: Comes from the *onscreen* world – the characters can hear it (dialogue, telephone).

NON-DIEGETIC: Comes from *outside* the onscreen world - only the audience hears it (narration, voice-over).

UNIT 1: POPULAR CULTURE TEXTS: NARRATIVE GROUP METHOD LAB (100 POINTS)

Objectives:

- To describe the popular culture texts from a Communication Studies perspective and to define and utilize media analysis terms.
- To analyze the power of popular culture texts' power to represent and shape social power and cultural identities.

Student Learning Outcomes:

Students will be able to

- Identify the given pop culture text's terms of analysis.
- Explain symbolism and intertextuality as it relates to the given pop culture text.

Description: In this assignment, your group will be introduced to the basic grammar of textual analysis on an assigned text. First, your group will label the following terms for the given text. Second, your group will then pick a symbol within the text and do a five step symbolic analysis. Finally, you will find two examples of intertextuality within the given text and label what type of intertextuality is being illustrated.

Terms

Genre	Conflict	Master Plot	Point of View	Protagonist
Antagonist	Foil	Minor Characters	Archetype for the protagonist	

Archetype for the antagonist

Symbolic Analysis - 5 steps

1. Pick a symbol that is visible and tangible.
2. Did you pick the symbol because of its intensity, prominence, and/or repetition?
3. What does the symbol reflect within the text?
4. What is the importance of the symbol?
5. What are common uses of symbol outside of the text?

Find **two examples** of intertextuality within the text and label what type of intertextuality was illustrated.

GRADING RUBRIC— UNIT 1: NARRATIVE GROUP METHOD LAB

	Exemplary	Proficient	Developing	Beginning
Pop Culture Text Terms 20 points	All terms labeled correctly in given text. (20–18 points)	Most terms labeled correctly in given text. (17–16 points)	Some terms labeled correctly in given text. (15–14 points).	Few terms labeled correctly in given text. (13–0 points).
Symbolic Analysis 30 points	Chosen symbol and analysis demonstrate an advanced understanding of text. (30–27 points).	Chosen symbol and analysis demonstrate a competent understanding of text. (26–24 points).	Chosen symbol and analysis demonstrate a cursory understanding of text. (23–21 points).	Chosen symbol and analysis demonstrate a incomplete of text. (20–0 points).
Intertextuality 30 points	Both examples establish expertise of intertextuality in pop culture text. (30–27 points).	Both examples establish knowledge of intertextuality in pop culture text. (26–24 points).	At least one example establishes some knowledge of intertextuality in pop culture text. (23–21 points).	Neither example establishes ample knowledge of intertextuality in pop culture text. (20–0 points).
Mechanics 20 points	Few to no distracting errors in spelling, grammar, or mechanics. (20–18 points).	Some distracting errors in spelling, grammar, or mechanics. (17–16 points).	Several distracting errors in spelling, grammar, or mechanics. (15–14 points).	Too many distracting errors to be considered a final draft. (13–0 points).

Points: _____ /100

NARRATIVE GROUP METHOD LAB: TERMS & DEFINITIONS

Genre: A specific type of popular culture text which shares a characteristic set of conventions in style, subject matter, themes, and values.

1. Comedy	5. Fantasy	9. Thriller	13. Horror	17. Documentary
2. Drama	6. Musical	10. Mystery	14. Serial	18. Reality
3. Western	7. Action	11. Procedural	15. Urban	19. Soap Opera
4. Sci/Fi	8. Adventure	12. Crime	16. Erotic	20. Romance

Conflict: The central struggle between two forces (overall struggle, not one scene). Creates **plot** using timeless and universal issues.

   – Character vs. _____ (self; character; society; nature)

Plot: Sequence of events (What happens in the story). **NOT** a summary. There are a list of master plots below.

Point of View: *Who* tells the story (narrative voice) and *how* the story is told (*narrative perspective – i.e., the point of view of the camera*)

- **1st person:** Narrator is a character within the story - "*I*" (or, when plural, "*we*")
- **3rd person:** Narrator is an unspecified entity or uninvolved person that conveys the story, but not a character within the story. Every character is referred to by the narrator as "*he, she, it,* or *they*" but never as "*I*" or "*we.*" Most images/moving pictures are from 3rd person perspective.
- **Other:** 2nd person (YOU are a character); Alternating POV; Music as narrator, etc.

   Protagonist – Main character

   Antagonist – Opposes the protagonist

   Foil – Contrast to the protagonist

Minor characters – Lack depth because they have only 1-2 qualities that are either all *good* or *bad* and do not change during the story

Archetype – The *original* model for characters after which other characters are patterned.

What symbol is present in the text?

- Give an example of something you see that is a symbol. Only select **one** item.
- Look for something visible / tangible.
  - Arrangement, prominence, names, props, shapes/lines, colors

Why do you believe it is a symbol?

- Is it privileged through <u>intensity</u>, <u>prominence</u>, and/or <u>repetition</u>? How so?
  o At least one of <u>intensity</u>, <u>prominence</u>, and/or <u>repetition</u> should be given as your answer.

What does the symbol reflect?

- A symbol is a sign for something else. What does this symbol mean?

Why is this symbol important to *this* text?

- Why was it included in the text? "So what"?

[How] Is this a common symbol *outside* of this text?

- Have you seen it in other texts? If so, where else?
- How does it exist outside of this text (in everyday life)?

Intertextuality: The way texts refer to other texts.

Intextual Analysis

I. *Trace:* **What does this text remind you of (in pop culture)?**
- Always ask of a text, "What does this remind me of?"
- No direct mention, or even indirect allusion, was made, but something about the text reminds you of another text (based on the narrative elements) or a real-life event.
- Can be intentional or unintentional (coincidental)

   [**Example:**] The monster and the rustling of the trees on the first episode of *LOST* reminds you of the new *King Kong* (which reminds you of *Jurassic Park,* which makes you think of *Jaws*).

II. **Does this text *directly mention* any other pop culture artifacts by name? Which ones?***
- Television shows, movies, books, songs, websites, performers, etc.
- You would "get it" if you knew of the other artifact, even if you hadn't seen it
- Intentional

   [**Example:**] When Michael Scott mentions the singer Lady Gaga during *The Office*

III. **Does this text have an *indirect allusion* to another text? Which ones?***
- You would only get it if you had seen the other text
- Intentional

   [**Example:**] On the first episode of *Cougar Town*, when Jules Cobb is hung over and we see a photo slide show of her previous night, it is just like the photo slide show in *The Hangover*. If you hadn't seen *The Hangover*, you wouldn't get the reference.

   A. **If so, what form did this allusion take?**
   - Intentional
     o **Easter Eggs** – Items intentionally hidden in the text by the creators simply for fun – When Buzz Lightyear peaks through the bushes in *Toy Story 2* and the characters from *A Bug's Life* are standing on the branch.
     o **"Winks"/ "Nods"** – When Barney (Neil Patrick Harris) finishes an episode of *How I Met Your Mother* by typing on an old, blue-screen computer, it is a clear nod to his time starring on *Doogie Howser, MD*
     o **Satire** – When *The Simpson's* makes critical commentary on sitcoms and family life
     o **Parodies** – When *The Family Guy* makes an exaggerated episode based on *Star Wars*
   - **Re-enactments** – When Princess Fiona in *Shrek* uses the same martial arts moves and special effects as Trinity on *The Matrix*

IV. **What did you think about the use of this intertextuality?**
- Does the intertextuality detract from or add to the text (short-term or long-term)?
- Why did this text use intertextuality?
  o To connect with/relate to the audience?
  o For humor (e.g., as an inside joke?)?
  o To add enjoyment for the viewer?
  o To make the text seem relevant/current for the time?

*****NOTE:** *Though Product Placement and Product Integration can be considered intertextuality, they are part of their* <u>*own*</u> *category of analysis*

NARRATIVE GROUP METHOD LAB: ADDITIONAL TERMS (FOR YOUR REFERENCE)

Master Plots*

– Write in examples that come to your mind as you look over the list of Master Plots.

1. **Quest**: Search for a person, place or thing (tangible or not). Looking for something that will signify change in her life. Mental or emotional quest.

   a. *Little Miss Sunshine, Don Quixote, Wizard of Oz, Harry Potter*

   Your examples:_____

2. **Adventure**: The focus is not on the person (as in "Quest") but in the journey itself. Physical adventure.

   a. *Dumb & Dumber, The Mummy, Master & Commander, Into the Wild*

   Your examples:_____

3. **Pursuit**: One character chases another.

   a. *Jaws, Terminator, Alien, Halloween, The Fugitive, Hunt for the Red October*

   Your examples:_____

4. **Rescue**: Hero must go forth (similar to "Adventure") and chase the antagonist (similar to "Pursuit") but depends on a third person, the victim.

   a. *The Golden Child, Saving Private Ryan, Finding Nemo, Star Wars (IV)*

   Your examples:_____

5. **Escape**: Hero confined (physically) against will and wants to escape.

   a. *The Shawshank Redemption; Count of Monte Cristo, Escape from NY*

   Your examples:_____

6. **Revenge**: Retaliation by hero against the villain for real or imagined injury.

   a. *Kill Bill, Sin City, Memento, Death Wish, Rambo*

   Your examples:_____

7. **The Riddle**: Has morphed into the "Mystery" genre – a "whodunit" challenge to the hero / audience to solve the puzzle.

   a. *The Da Vinci Code, The Usual Suspects, National Treasure*

   Your examples:_____

8. **Rivalry**: Competing for the same object or goal as another character. Parity. The unstoppable force verses the immovable object.

   a. *Grumpy Old Men, Jason-Freddy, Alien-Predator, Godzilla-King Kong*

   Your examples:_____

9. **Underdog**: Subset of "Rivalry." The hero is disadvantaged by overwhelming odds. Uneven match.

   a. *Rocky, The Karate Kid, Billy Elliot, Hoosiers, Rudy*

   Your examples:_____

---

*Adapted from *20 Master Plots: And How to Build Them* by Ronald B. Tobias.

10. **Temptation:** The frailty of human nature. Opportunities to be stupid, wrong, immoral, or illegal (against our better judgment).

    a. *Unfaithful, Out of Sight, The Last Temptation of Christ, Matchpoint, Basic Instinct*

    Your examples:_____

11. **Metamorphosis:** Physical change – the character literally changes shape.

    a. *The Fly, Dracula, Beauty & The Beast, Robocop, Big*

    Your examples:_____

12. **Transformation:** Related to metamorphosis. Process of mental or emotional change as hero journeys through something. Usually it is an adult changing.

    a. *The Matrix, Total Recall*

    Your examples:_____

13. **Maturation:** Similar to both **Metamorphosis** & **Transformation**. Character changes for the better. "Coming of age" stories (children becoming adults).

    a. *Stand By Me, Breakfast Club, The Outsiders, 16 Candles*

    Your examples:_____

14. **Love:** Lovers finding each other... but… obstacles keep lovers from consummating the affair until the ultimate, joyous (re)union.

    a. *Ghost, Splash, Chasing Amy, Pretty Woman*

    Your examples:_____

15. **Forbidden Love:** Love that crosses the line of social taboos (race, religion, class).

    a. *Titanic, Romeo & Juliet, Monster's Ball, Jungle Fever, King Kong*

    Your examples:_____

16. **Sacrifice:** Offer an object to establish a good relationship between hero and _____ (not always a god… sometimes it is love, honor, charity, humanity).

    a. *Can't Buy Me Love, Just One of the Guys, Boys Don't Cry*

    Your examples:_____

17. **Discovery:** Pursuit of learning, quest to find out who hero "is."

    a. *Dead Poets Society, Finding Forester, Freedom Writers*

    Your examples:_____

18. **Wretched Excess:** Pushing the limits of acceptable behavior. Extreme, fringe, excessive.

    a. *Othello, Wall Street, Leaving Las Vegas, Training Day, The Machinist*

    Your examples:_____

19. & 20. **Ascension** & **Descension:** The rise & fall of the hero.

    a. *Boogie Nights, Blow, Scarface, Goodfellas, E True Hollywood Story*

    Your examples:_____

Hero's Journey—*Write in examples that come to your mind as you look over the structure of the Hero's Journey.*

This is a brief overview of Joseph Campbell / Christopher Vogler's "Hero's Journey," which explains how many of these **Master Plots** are structured and arranged. Adapted from *The Writer's Journey: Mythic Structure for Writers* by Christopher Vogler

BASIC STRUCTURE:

1. Heroes are introduced in the **ORDINARY WORLD**, where
2. they receive the **CALL TO ADVENTURE.**
3. They are **RELUCTANT** at first or **REFUSE THE CALL**, but
4. are encouraged by a **MENTOR** to
5. **CROSS THE FIRST THRESHOLD** and enter the *Special World*, where
6. they encounter **TESTS, ALLIES, AND ENEMIES.**
7. They **APPROACH THE INMOST CAVE**, crossing a second threshold
8. where they endure the **ORDEAL.**
9. They take possession of their **REWARD** (the *sword*) and
10. are pursued on **THE ROAD BACK** to the *Ordinary World*.
11. They cross the third threshold, experience a **RESURRECTION**, and are transformed by the experience.
12. They **RETURN WITH THE ELIXER**, a boon or treasure to benefit the *Ordinary World*.

EXAMPLES:

1. **Ordinary world** – Luke Skywalker bored on the farm; Frodo in his Shire; Harry Potter in London; Simba in his kingdom; Dorothy in Kansas

   Your examples:_____

2. **Call to adventure** – Obi Wan Kenobi asks Luke Skywalker to help him; Gandalf tells Frodo to leave the Shire; Hagrid gathers Harry Potter; Simba is banished by Scar; the tornado takes Dorothy from Kansas.

   Your examples:_____

3. **Refusal of the call (reluctant hero)** – Luke refuses to go with Kenobi until his aunt and uncle are killed; Neo refuses to believe Morpheus about the matrix

   Your examples:_____

4. **Mentor (wise elder)** – Morpheus; Mr. Miyagi; Yoda; Gandalf; Glinda the Good Witch

   Your examples:_____

5. **Crossing the first threshold (hero commits to the journey)** – Neo takes the pill; Axel Foley defies his boss in Beverly Hills Cop; Luke enters the bar on Tatooine; Harry boards the train.
6. **Tests, Allies, Enemies** – Luke meets Han Solo in a bar; Harry meets Ron and Hermione on a train; Dorothy meets people on the Yellow Brick Road; Simba meets Timon and Pumba.

   Your examples:_____

7. **Approach the inmost** cave – Luke is sucked into the Death Star; Frodo enters the mountain; Neo arrives in the womb inside reality

   Your examples:_____

8. **The ordeal (will she/he live or die?)** – Luke is getting crushed by a trash compactor; Neo gets unplugged and slips into water; Simba takes on Scar.

    Your examples:_____

9. **Reward (Seizing the "sword")** – Indiana Jones finds the treasure; Neo grasps his powers; Frodo gets rid of the ring.

    Your examples:_____

10. **The road back** – Luke is pursued back across the galaxy by Darth Vader; Elliot and E.T. "fly" on their bike back to the meeting ground

    Your examples:_____

11. **Resurrection (the hero must face one last desperate shot from death)** – Frodo is trapped and dying in hot lava; Luke must escape from the Death Star; Harry Potter must survive a deception from Voldemort

    Your examples:_____

12. **Return with the "elixir"** – Dorothy returns home knowing there is no place like home; E.T. returns home with human friendship; Harry Potter returns home confident and knowing magic; Frodo returns with an extraordinary story for ordinary hobbits.

    Your examples:_____

Types of Archetypes:

Adapted from: Cowden, T., LaFever, C., and Viders, S. (2000) *The Complete Writer's Guide to Heroes and Heroines.* (www.tamicowden.com)

– *Write in examples that come to your mind as you look over the list of Archetypes.*
   I. **Heroes:**
   - *The Chief*: dynamic leader, nothing but work.
     o Obi Wan Kenobi, *Star Wars*; Captain Kirk, *Star Trek*; Jack, *Lost*, Nick Fury, *The Avengers*

       Your examples:_____

   - *The Bad Boy:* the rebel, walks on the wild side
     o Han Solo, *Star Wars*; James Stark, *Rebel Without a Cause*; Sawyer, *Lost;* Tony Stark, *Iron Man*; Wolverine, *X-men*

       Your examples:_____

   - *The Best Friend:* Sweet, safe, and never lets anyone down
     o Chewbacca, *Star Wars*; Chandler, *Friends*; Marshall, *How I Met Your Mother;* Ron, *Harry Potter*

       Your examples:_____

   - *The Charmer:* Fun, irresistible, smooth operator; not too dependable
     o Lando Calrissian, *The Empire Strikes Back*; Joey, *Friends*; Barney, *How I Met Your Mother*

       Your examples:_____

   - *The Lost Soul:* Tortured, secretive, brooding, and unforgiving; sensitive & vulnerable
     o Beast, *Beauty & Beast*; Shrek, *Shrek*; Mulder, *X-Files*, Bruce Banner/Hulk, *The Incredible Hulk*

       Your examples:_____

- *The Professor*: Cool & analytical; knows every answer; logical, introverted, inflexible
  - Yoda, *Star Wars*; Spock, *Star Trek*; Professor Xavier, *X-Men*

    Your examples:_____

- *The Swashbuckler*: Adventurer, physical and daring; action, action, action
  - Indiana Jones, *Raiders of the Lost Ark*; Jack Sparrow, *Pirates of the Caribbean*; Thor, *Thor*

    Your examples:_____

- *Warrior:* The noble champion; the knight in shining armor, reluctant hero; champion of the underdog; honorable and relentless
  - William Wallace, *Braveheart*; Harry, *Harry Potter*; Mikael Blomkvist, *Girl With the Dragon Tattoo*; Steve Rogers, *Captain America*

    Your examples:_____

II. **Heroines**
- *The Boss:* a go-getter, climbs the ladder of success, demands respect
  - Princess Leia, *Star Wars*; Erin Brockovich, *Erin Brockovich*; Miranda Bailey, *Grey's Anatomy*; Rayna James, *Nashville*

    Your examples:_____

- *The Seductress:* Enchantress, gets her way, mysterious & manipulative
  - Vianne, *Chocolat;* Giacinta "Jinx" Johnson, *Die Another Day (James Bond),* Black Widow, *The Avengers*

    Your examples:_____

- *The Spunky Kid:* Gutsy and true
  - Samantha, *Bewitched,* Mary Richards, *Mary Tyler Moore*; Sookie, *True Blood/Sookie Stackhouse Book Series*; Scarlett O'Connor, *Nashville*

    Your examples:_____

- *The Free Spirit*: Eternal optimist, dances to her own tune, playful
  - Lucy, *I Love Lucy*; Jess, *New Girl*; Cher Horowitz, *Clueless*

    Your examples:_____

- *The Waif:* The original damsel in distress, child-like innocence
  - Dorothy, *Wizard of Oz*; Buttercup, *The Princess Bride*; Brittany, *Glee*; Bella, *Twilight*

    Your examples:_____

- *The Librarian:* Controlled and clever, prim & proper, yet passionate
  - Scully, *X-Files*; Marion Paroo, *The Music Man* (literally a librarian); Rachel, *Glee*; Pepper Potts, *Iron Man*

    Your examples:_____

- *The Crusader:* Dedicated fighter, kicks butt and takes names
  - Buffy, *Buffy the Vampire Slayer,* Ripley, *Alien*; Lisbeth Salander, *Girl With a Dragon Tattoo,* Katniss, *Hunger Games*

    Your examples:_____

- *The Nurturer*: Serene, capable, takes care of everything
  - o Marge Simpson, *The Simpsons*; Mary Poppins, *Mary Poppins*; Aunt May, *Spiderman*; Jane Nichols, *27 Dresses*

    Your examples:_____

III. Villains (Male)

- *The Tyrant*: Bullying despot, ruthless ruler
  - o Darth Vader, *Star Wars*; Ming the Merciless, *Flash Gordon*; Voldemort, *Harry Potter*; David Karofsky, *Glee*

    Your examples:_____

- *The Outcast*: Tortured and unforgiving; redemption at any cost
  - o Grinch, *How the Grinch Stole Christmas*; Norman Bates, *Psycho*; Sylar, *Heroes*; Smeagol/Gollum, *Lord of the Rings*

    Your examples:_____

- *The Devil*: The charming fiend, preys on people's moral weaknesses
  - o John Milton, *The Devil's Advocate*; Thomas Barrow, *Downton Abbey*; Dracula, *Dracula*; Jigsaw, Saw

    Your examples:_____

- *The Evil Genius*: the malevolent mastermind, elaborate puzzles and experiments
  - o Emporer Palpatine, *Return of the Jedi*; Lex Luthor, *Superman*; Hannibal Lecter, *The Silence of the Lambs*; Magneto, *X-Men*

    Your examples:_____

IV. Villains (Female)

- *The Black Widow*: Lures victims into her web, uses charms to get her way
  - o Cat Woman, *Batman*; Santana and Quinn, *Glee*; Mystique, *X-Men*; Emma, *The Following*

    Your examples:_____

- *The Lunatic*: Madwoman, draws others into her crazy environment
  - o Alex Forrest (Glenn Close), *Fatal Attraction*; "Mr. Yang," *Psych*; Bellatrix Lestrange, *Harry Potter*

    Your examples:_____

- *The "Bitch"*: Lies, cheats, and steals her way to the top
  - o Evil Stepmother, *Cinderella*; Cruella Deville, *101 Dalmatian*; Kitty, *Glee*; Regina, *Mean Girls*

    Your examples:_____

- The Schemer: Lethal plotter, she plans the demise of others
  - o Wicked Witch, *The Wizard of Oz*; Kathryn, *Cruel Intentions*; Sue Sylvester, *Glee*; Victoria, *Twilight Saga*

    Your examples:_____

UNIT 2: POPULAR CULTURE INDUSTRIES

Who makes popular culture texts, and why? Like most things Americans buy—from food to clothing to cars—movies, music, video games, and television shows are made by large companies who strive to sell their goods for a profit. Unlike other consumer items, however, popular culture texts often arrive onscreen having had to blend their commercial motivations with creative ones. It's this unique balance of art and commerce that makes close study of popular culture so important. In the first unit, we acquired some terminology for describing cultural texts' artistic expressions. In this unit, students will examine more closely the organizations, work routines, and ideas that make cultural creation a profitable enterprise. As Jennifer Holt and Alisa Perren note:

> The study of media industries is a varied and diverse project...Discourses in the trade papers, the popular press, and academic publications are supplemented by writing in digital communities, online journals and the blogosphere. This range of perspectives is both a necessary component and constitutive element of this work; after all, to explore media industries in the twenty-first century is to engage with an extraordinary range of texts, markets, economies, artistic traditions, business models, cultural policies, technologies, regulations, and creative expression.[2]

Examining the industries that create pop culture is one major component to understanding that cultural meanings don't come just from what we see onscreen. In Unit 3, we'll continue looking beyond pop culture texts themselves to the various social and historical contexts out of which they emerge.

---

[2]Holt, Jennifer and Alisa Perren, "Introduction: Does the World Really Need One More Field of Study?" in Jennifer Holt and Alisa Perren (eds), *Media Industries: History, Theory, and Method.* Malden, MA: Wiley-Blackwell, 2009, 1.

UNIT 2: POPULAR CULTURE INDUSTRIES

POP CULTURE PITCH: INDUSTRY INSIDER REPORT & PRESENTATION (50 POINTS EACH)

Objectives:

- To describe the popular culture texts from a Communication Studies perspective and to define and utilize key media analysis terms.
- To analyze the industries that produce popular culture texts.

Student Learning Outcomes:

Students will be able to

- Research and synthesize main ideas from primary documents for a given popular culture industry text, trend, or practice.
- Research and describe the current climate of culture industries.
- Describe the ideological implications of culture as a commercial enterprise.

Description: In this assignment, your group will analyze **primary documents** in order to better understand the strategies of the commercial industries that create popular culture. Primary documents are ones created either directly by those working in a culture industry (such as production notes from a film's director), or by trade publications that cover the day-to-day operations of an industry (such as *Variety, The Hollywood Reporter,* and *AdWeek*). Major daily newspapers such as *The New York Times* and *The Wall Street Journal* also have reporters dedicated to following the media industry "beat." In any form, primary documents are comprised of factual, first-hand accounts of popular culture industry developments as they happen, not on second-hand opinions about them.

Groups will be divided into two categories–**popular culture creatives and executives**. Creatives are artists—the writers, directors, and performers who generate original cultural material. Executives are business people who work for a media company comprised of the producers, distributors, and advertisers who strive to profit from cultural products. Over the course of the unit, **creatives** will be responsible for developing a film or television show (per your instructor's directions), with one group for each of the following genres that you learned about in Unit 1: **comedy, drama, action/thriller, horror/fantasy, reality**. In order to do so, creatives will analyze primary documents and answer the following questions:

1. **Industry Insider Report:** What **recent** examples of texts from your genre have proven popular or successful, and why? Select **4–5 (per your instructor)** recent examples, using at least **two** primary documents to discuss each (8–10 total primary documents), and compose an executive summary of your findings. What dominant ideologies do these examples embody? How does discussion of these texts in your trade articles address a given ideology?
2. **Pitch Meeting:** Give the "elevator pitch" for your show or movie, including its tagline and plot overview. Does your new show or movie undermine or support the dominant ideology of your genre? Does it do both?

Meanwhile, **executives** will be responsible for researching their respective media company (per your instructor's directions). Options include: **Netflix, Disney, Time Warner, Comcast,** and **NewsCorp**. In order to do so, **executives** will examine primary documents and answer the following questions:

1. **Industry Insider Report:** Give an overview of your media conglomerate, including its ownership and component companies. What **recent** examples of texts from your company have proven popular or successful, and why? Select **4–5 (per your instructor)** recent examples, using at least **two** primary documents to discuss each (8–10 total primary documents).

2. **Pitch Meeting:** Give the "elevator pitch" for your company. With what dominant ideologies does your media company generally align? What types of popular culture texts might it produce to undermine these ideologies?

At the end of the unit, creatives will pitch their ideas to the class in 10 minute presentations. The following class, executives will pitch to the class their company overviews in 10 minute presentations. Before the following class, each creatives group will rank their desired outlet, and each executives group will rank their sought-after film or program.

Presentation Guidelines – All good presentations have an introduction and a conclusion.

Executives – focus on 1 television channel, 1 film production company, and 2 other major holdings of your conglomerate. Use a PowerPoint presentation to illustrate your main points. (Netflix focus on 1 television show, 1 movie, and 2 other texts of your choice that are iconic to Netflix).

Creatives – focus on the elements of successful texts within your genre, then pitch your text and explain how it follows or challenges these elements.

Industry Insider Report Guidelines – Due at the time of your presentation. This documents should be typed, double spaced, and two to four pages in length. Answer the questions under your group's description.

Bibliography – Each group is required to generate a bibliography citing their primary sources used in the Industry Insider Report.

Creatives' Worksheet

Text Genre:_____   Group Members:_____

Rank the 4 companies in order of preference for your text, with number 1 being the best fit, number 4 the worst fit.

1._____   3._____

2._____   4._____

Company 1:_____

What fits best about this company for your text?

What doesn't fit about this company for your text?

Company 2:_____

What fits best about this company for your text?

What doesn't fit about this company for your text?

Company 3:_____

What fits best about this company for your text?

What doesn't fit about this company for your text?

Company 4:_____

What fits best about this company for your text?

What doesn't fit about this company for your text?

Executives' Worksheet

Company's Name:_____   Group Members:_____

Rank the 4 texts in order of preference for your Company, with number 1 being the best fit, number 4 the worst fit.

1._____   3._____

2._____   4._____

Creative Text 1 Title:_____   Genre:_____

What fits best from this text for your network?

What doesn't fit from this text for your network?

Creative Text 2 Title:_____   Genre:_____

What fits best from this text for your network?

What doesn't fit from this text for your network?

Creative Text 3 Title:_____   Genre:_____

What fits best from this text for your network?

What doesn't fit from this text for your network?

Creative Text 4 Title:_____   Genre:_____

What fits best from this text for your network?

What doesn't fit from this text for your network?

GRADING RUBRIC— POP CULTURE PITCH: INDUSTRY INSIDER REPORT (50 POINTS)

	Exemplary	Proficient	Developing	Beginning
Content 30 points	Industry report clearly illustrates the ideologies with supporting evidence of primary documents. (30–27 points).	Industry report somewhat illustrates the ideologies with supporting evidence of primary documents. (26–24 points).	Industry report struggles to illustrates the ideologies with supporting evidence of primary documents. (23–21 points).	Industry report does not highlight ideologies or use does not use supporting evidence of primary documents. (20–0 points).
MLA format 10 points	Correct formatting used for in-text citations and works cited page. (10–9 points).	Mostly correct formatting used for in-text citations and works cited page. (8 points).	Several errors in formatting used for in-text citations and works cited page. (7 points).	Too many incorrect formatting used for in-text citations and works cited page. (6–0 points).
Mechanics 10 points	Few to no distracting errors in spelling, grammar, or mechanics. (10–9 points).	Some distracting errors in spelling, grammar, or mechanics. (8 points).	Several distracting errors in spelling, grammar, or mechanics. (7 points).	Too many distracting errors to be considered a final draft. (6–0 points).

GRADING RUBRIC— POP CULTURE PITCH: PRESENTATION (50 POINTS)

	Exemplary	Proficient	Developing	Beginning
Delivery 10 points	All speakers excel at all aspect of delivery, including eye contact, vocal variety and gestures. (10–9 points).	Most of the speakers excel at all aspect of delivery, including eye contact, vocal variety and gestures. (8 points).	Some of the speakers excel at some of the aspect of delivery, including eye contact, vocal variety and gestures. (7 points).	None of the speakers excel at delivery including eye contact, vocal variety and gestures (6–0 points).
Content 30 points	Explanation of industry and company is thorough, based on communication studies theory, and supported with researched evidence. (30–27 points).	Most explanation of industry and company is thorough, based on communication studies theory, and supported with researched evidence. (26–24 points).	Some explanation of industry and company is thorough, based on communication studies theory, and supported with researched evidence. More thorough explanation needed. (23–21 points).	More thorough explanation of industry and company is necessary. Very little of included explanation is based on communication studies theory or supported with researched evidence. (20–0 points).
Format 10 points	Presentation follows a logical sequence that flows well between ideas: introduction, thesis, body with supporting evidence, and a well-developed conclusion. (10–9 points).	Presentation follows a logical sequence that mostly flows between ideas: introduction, thesis, body, and conclusion. (8 points).	Presentation follows a somewhat logical sequence: introduction, thesis, body with supporting evidence, conclusion. Some issues with clarity, or flow. (7 points).	Presentation is lacking either an introduction or conclusion and there is little clarity of main idea and little flow between ideas. (6–0 points).

UNIT 3: POPULAR CULTURE & HISTORICAL CONTEXT

Does a popular culture text reflect the social values and historical events of its time or help to create them? By the end of Unit 3, students will discover that the answer to this question is, "Both." In the previous two units, we considered how the competing tensions of art and commerce manifest in popular culture. In this unit, students will examine the dialogue between popular culture texts and the social and cultural circumstances out of which they are produced. Doing so will help us see that studying cultural history actually involves analyzing both historical events themselves and the ways that we talk and write about those events. As Michele Hilmes notes:

> Thus history is not the mere writing down of static, dead events in a fixed chronology. Rather, it is a continuous and interactive process, constantly taken up, shaken up, revised, and utilized by people in the here and now…we'll examine the ways our culture devised to think about this new set of phenomena: the discursive patterns that encouraged thinking and talking about [popular culture] in some ways and not others, and the hopes and fears that engendered them.[3]

Grappling with the historical context of your chosen pop culture text will provide as complete a picture of its many meanings as possible before finally considering, in Unit 4, popular culture's audiences and technologies.

---

[3]Hilmes, Michele, *Only Connect: A Cultural History of Broadcasting in the United States*. Boston, MA: Wadsworth, 2014, 15.

UNIT 3: HISTORICAL CONTEXT METHOD LABS (150 POINTS)

(Students pick ONE of the following three options to write about: race/ethnicity, gender, or sexuality)

Objectives:

- To describe the popular culture texts from a Communication Studies perspective and to define and utilize key media analysis terms.
- To analyze the power of popular culture text to represent and shape social power and cultural identities.
- To explain the relationship between popular culture texts and the socio-historical contexts.

Student Learning Outcomes:

Students will be able to

- Identify and describe the key socio-historical contexts out of which your text emerges.
- Describe how your assigned text represents the conflicts of its socio-historical context.

Race, Gender or Sexuality Method Lab Assignment Guidelines: In this assignment, students will view the assigned pop cultural text from your instructor and use key media analysis terms to compose a 2–3 page essay that answers the following question: What is the relationship between this text's representations of (race/ethnicity, gender, sexuality) and its historical contexts? In discussing your answer, use at least **1 (one)** scholarly resource in supporting your answer, and cite it according to MLA style.

Questions to guide your thinking: (DO NOT ANSWER IN YOUR PAPER)

- Who is the protagonist? How do you know this? Discuss using terminology from Unit 1.
- What is the protagonist's (race/ethnicity, gender, sexuality)? What is the relationship of the protagonist to the other representations of (race/ethnicity, gender, sexuality) in the text?
- Describe each character's values within the representations of the (race/ethnicity, gender, sexuality) in the text.
- What is the more recent social context of your text?
- What historical context informs the representations of (race/ethnicity, gender, sexuality) in your text? You can discuss material from lecture, material your group used in the poster session, or material from your own research.

GRADING RUBRIC—UNIT 3: HISTORICAL CONTEXT METHOD LAB: 150 POINTS

	Exemplary	Proficient	Developing	Beginning
Socio-historic context of text 30 points	Socio-historic context is clearly identified, accurate, and relevant text. (30–27 points).	Socio-historic context mostly represented between the text and social movements at the time. (26–24 points).	Socio-historic context loosely linked between the text and the social movements at the time. (23–21 points).	Socio-historic context is not represented between the text and the social movements at the time. (20–0 points).
Supporting Evidence 30 points	Explanation of socio-historic context is thorough, based on communication studies theory, and supported with researched evidence. (30–27 points).	Most explanation of socio-historic context is thorough, based on communication studies theory, and supported with researched evidence. (26–24 points).	Some explanation of socio-historic context is thorough, based on communication studies theory, and supported with researched evidence. More thorough explanation needed. (23–21 points).	More thorough explanation of socio-historic context is necessary. Very little of included explanation is based on communication studies theory or supported with researched evidence. (20–0 points).
Writing 50 points	Writing follows a logical sequence that flows well between ideas: introduction, thesis, body with supporting evidence, and a well-developed conclusion. (50–45 points).	Writing follows a logical sequence that mostly flows between ideas: introduction, thesis, body, and conclusion. (44–40 points).	Writing follows a somewhat logical sequence: introduction, thesis, body with supporting evidence, conclusion. Some issues with clarity, or flow. (39–35 points).	Some writing follows a logical sequence but there is little clarity of main idea and little flow between ideas. (34–0 points).
MLA format 20 points	Correct formatting used for in-text citations and works cited page. (20–18 points).	Mostly correct formatting used for in-text citations and works cited page. (17–16 points).	Several errors in formatting used for in-text citations and works cited page. (15–14 points).	Too many incorrect formatting used for in-text citations and works cited page. (13–0 points).
Mechanics 20 points	Few to no distracting errors in spelling, grammar, or mechanics. (20–18 points).	Some distracting errors in spelling, grammar, or mechanics. (17–16 points).	Several distracting errors in spelling, grammar, or mechanics. (15–14 points).	Too many distracting errors to be considered a final draft. (13–0 points).

UNIT 4: POPULAR CULTURE AUDIENCES & TECHNOLOGIES

The last critical lens through which we can understand popular culture is how it is received. More often than not, popular culture texts are viewed in large numbers by audiences who access them on an increasingly diverse array of electronic devices. More and more, it seems, our time is spent on the receiving end of some mediated cultural message. As Matt Hills notes:

> We are now audiences more of the time, whether this involves reading news about TV shows or film franchises we follow via social media, tweeting and blogging about our favored media consumption and fan objects, watching trailers via YouTube, or so on.[4]

Watching cultural texts isn't simply a passive experience, but can inspire a vast range of interpretations, activities, and uses. In the final unit of this course, students will consider their own role in creating popular culture's meanings, as well as how this process functions through specific technologies. Students will synthesize these thoughts with ideas and terms from the first three units in composing their final papers and projects.

---

[4]Hills, Matt, "Audience" in Laurie Ouellette and Jonathan Gray (eds), *Keywords for Media Studies*. New York: NYU Press, 2017, 18.

ANNOTATED BIBLIOGRAPHY (100 POINTS)

Objectives:

- To describe the popular culture texts from a Communication Studies perspective and to define and utilize key media analysis terms.
- To analyze the power of popular culture texts to represent and shape social power and cultural identities.
- To critique and construct arguments about popular culture and/as communication through research, writing, and civic or cultural engagement.

Student Learning Outcomes:

Students will be able to

- Find and analyze secondary scholarly sources that support a research question
- Cite a source in APA or MLA format
- Summarize and assess a scholarly source
- Utilize a scholarly source as evidence in support of an argument.

Pick a Topic

Description: In this assignment, you will read and analyze at least **five scholarly sources** that can be used in support of the argument of your final paper. Scholarly sources are secondary, interpretive accounts of cultural phenomena, as opposed to primary documents' contemporaneous accounts of industries. Scholarly sources are written by expert researchers in the fields of media and culture and are published in peer-reviewed journals or books. After processing your five sources, you will submit an annotated bibliography.

***At the top of your Annotated Bibliography write a draft of your **thesis** that the sources will be supporting. Submit an annotated bibliography of your best five sources on your topic in MLA Style. For each source, you will provide a description explaining why it should be useful to your project as described below.

An annotation is a summary and/or evaluation. Therefore, an annotated bibliography includes a summary and/ or evaluation of each of the sources. For your annotation on each source, include:

Paragraph 1 Summarize: What are the main arguments? What is the point of this book, article or source? What topics are covered? If someone asked what this source is about, what would you say?

Paragraph 2 Assess: After summarizing a source, it is helpful to evaluate it. How is it a useful source? How does it compare with other sources in your bibliography? Is the information reliable? Is this source biased or objective? What is the goal of this source?

Paragraph 3 Reflect: Once you've summarized and assessed a source, you need to ask how it fits into your research. Was this source helpful to you? How does it help you shape your argument? How can you use this source in your final project?

Consider organizing your annotated bibliography around the four units of media and popular culture analysis discussed in class thus far, though your sources do not have to cover all four units equally.

1. What elements of the **text** are most meaningful or significant, and how does the scholarly source support your observation?
2. What is your text's **industrial** context? What commercial forces does your scholarly source identify as affecting the creation of your text? Why is this significant?
3. What is the **historical** context out of which your text emerges? What are the key aspects of your text's context that your scholarly source identifies, and why are they significant?
4. Who is the intended **audience** of your text? How does your scholarly source characterize the way your text constructs its intended audience?

GRADING RUBRIC— ANNOTATED BIBLIOGRAPHY

	Exemplary	Proficient	Developing	Beginning
Annotations 50 points	5 annotations properly summarize, assess, and reflect the source. (50–45 point range)	4 out of 5 annotations properly summarize, assess, and reflect the sources. (44–40 range)	3 out of 5 annotations properly summarize, assess, and reflect the sources. (39–35 range)	2 or fewer annotations properly summarize, assess, and reflect the sources. (34–0 range)
Sources 20 points	All sources are credible scholarly sources that address the four analytic units. (20–18 range)	4 out of the 5 sources are credible scholarly sources that address the four analytic units. (17–16 range)	3 out of the 5 sources are credible scholarly sources that address the four analytic units. (15–14 range)	2 or fewer sources are credible scholarly sources that address the four analytic units. (13–0 range)
Format 20 points	Correct formatting used for the citations. (20–18 range)	Mostly correct formatting used for the citations. (17–16 range).	Several errors in formatting used for the citations. (15–14 range)	Too many errors in formatting of the citations. (13–0 range)
Mechanics 10 points	Few to no distracting errors in spelling, grammar, or mechanics. (10–9 points).	Some distracting errors in spelling, grammar, or mechanics. (8 points).	Several distracting errors in spelling, grammar, or mechanics. (7 points).	Too many distracting errors to be considered a final draft. (6–0 points).

FINAL ESSAY (200 POINTS)

Objectives:

- To critique and construct arguments about popular culture and/as communication through research, writing, and civic or cultural engagement.

Student Learning Outcomes:

Students will be able to

- Argue persuasively about the meaning of a pop cultural text
- Research and synthesize evidence from the industrial, historical, audience, and textual domains of their chosen topic and explain how they interact in support of the text's meaning

Assignment Guidelines: Your assignment is to write a 4–6 page double-spaced page essay responding to the prompts below. The essay should demonstrate a clear understanding of the material covered in class, including readings, lectures, discussions, and screenings, synthesizing and making connections among concepts in each. Keep in mind, however, that the paper should reflect your own argument, and should thus be more than just a collage of other people's thoughts.

Your paper should focus on the same topic you set forth in your Annotated Bibliography.

Your paper should use at least 3 primary or secondary sources to back up your argument with in text citations and a bibliography in MLA format.

Your paper should have a clear introduction, thesis statement, body, and conclusion. It should also show clear organization and proper sentence structure, and it should be free of grammatical and spelling errors. Proofread! Points will be taken off for poorly organized or sloppy writing.

- **THINK** about a pop culture or media text that interests you—consider, but don't limit yourself to: television, film, music, magazines, social networking sites, e-commerce sites, clothing, sports…
- **VIEW** as many iterations of your chosen text as you can, enough to be an expert on it. If it's a movie franchise, watch each entry. If it's a television show, watch several episodes of it. Take notes.
- **RE-READ** materials from your annotated bibliography. What sources help you better understand your chosen text(s)?
- **ANSWER** the following question: **Why does your chosen cultural text matter?** In doing so, address the four areas of popular cultural studies analysis—text, industry, historical context, and audience. Develop an argument that helps capture why you think your text matters, drawing an original position about your cultural text based on your viewings and readings. Consider: how do these areas interact in order to create your chosen text's meaning? What is that meaning? Describe it, and argue on its behalf.
- **ARGUE**, for example:
  o With its bleak, dystopian style and its place on niche-streaming network Hulu, *The Handmaid's Tale* calls progressive-minded viewers to action to address gender inequalities.
  o Although often dismissed as purely escapist, the *Fast & Furious* films bolster both Hollywood's renewed focus on franchises and on increasingly unconventional representations of mixed racial groups as "family."
- **GET STUCK**, or better yet, don't get stuck. Either way, come and see me anytime between now and the paper's due date for help. I will answer specific questions via email, too, but I will only read or comment on paper drafts in person with you.
- **UPLOAD YOUR PAPER TO CANVAS OR TURN IN A HARD COPY (PER YOUR INSTRUCTOR'S REQUEST)** no later than the start of class on its due date. Papers submitted late will be deducted 10% per calendar day late, starting at the beginning of class.

GRADING RUBRIC— FINAL ESSAY

	Exemplary	Proficient	Developing	Beginning
Position / Thesis 40 points	Presents an original and compelling thesis that uses the cultural studies model of text, industry, socio-historical context, and audience and how they interact in order to create its meaning. (40–36 points)	Presents a compelling thesis that uses the cultural studies model of text, industry, socio-historical context, and audience and how they interact in order to create its meaning. (35–32 points)	Presents a thesis that is broad or non-critical. It uses at least part of the cultural studies model of text, industry, socio-historical context, or audience (analysis and the idea of how they interact in order to create its meaning is unclear. (31–28 points)	Presents a thesis that does not demonstrate understanding of the cultural studies model of text, industry, socio-historical context, or audience. (27–0 points)
Argument/ Support 60 points	Provides a synthesized and seamless argument with critical, original ideas – by making a valid connection that was not already made in class. It is supported with well-chosen and meaningful evidence and successfully questions basic assumptions. (60–54 points)	Provides a convincing and clear argument that is supported with well-chosen and meaningful evidence, examples, and citations. Argument begins to make a valid connection that was not already made in class, but can be more developed or examined. (53–48 points)	Some of the argument is clear and convincing but some of it needs more evidence, examples, or citations and further analysis. Connections made are most likely expansions of what was discussed in class. (47–42 points)	Few of the arguments are clear and / or convincing. Needs more evidence, examples, and further analysis. Few connections are made between the argument and the support. (41–0 points)
Writing 60 points	Writing is focused on the thesis and follows a logical sequence – introduction, thesis, body with supporting evidence, conclusion – that flows well between paragraphs and ideas. A well-developed conclusion conveys an original and sophisticated closure to the argument. (60–54 points)	Most of the writing is focused on the thesis and follows a logical sequence – introduction, thesis, body with supporting evidence, conclusion – that flows well between paragraphs and ideas. A well-developed conclusion brings the reader back to the original argument and closes it. (53–48 points)	Some of the writing is focused on the thesis and follows a mostly logical sequence – introduction, thesis, body with supporting evidence, conclusion – but lacks flow between paragraphs and/or ideas. The conclusion restates the thesis and main supporting points. (47–42 points)	Writing is not focused on the thesis and does not follow a logical sequence throughout the essay. Ideas are written about separately and do not flow from one to the next. The conclusion simply restates the thesis. (41–0 points)
MLA format 20 points	Correct formatting used for in-text citations and works cited page. (20–18 points).	Mostly correct formatting used for in-text citations and works cited page. (17–16 points).	Several errors in formatting used for in-text citations and works cited page. (15–14 points).	Too many incorrect formatting used for in-text citations and works cited page. (13–0 points).
Mechanics 20 points	Few to no distracting errors in spelling, grammar, or mechanics. (20–18 points).	Some distracting errors in spelling, grammar, or mechanics. (17–16 points).	Several distracting errors in spelling, grammar, or mechanics. (15–14 points).	Too many distracting errors to be considered a final draft. (13–0 points).

FINAL EXAM: MUSEUM EXHIBIT POSTER (100 POINTS)

Objectives:
- To describe the popular culture texts from a Communication Studies perspective and to define and utilize key media analysis terms.
- To analyze the power of popular culture texts to represent and shape social power and cultural identities.
- To explain the relationship between popular culture texts and their socio-historical contexts.

Student Learning Outcomes:
Students will be able to

- Visually represent an historical pop culture case study through pictures and research.
- Describe the relationship between the histories of race, gender, or sexuality in the United States and their role in pop culture texts.

Description: For this assignment, your group will create a three panel, tri-fold poster that visually illustrates a popular culture text's relationship with its industrial and historical contexts. Your group may pick any popular culture case study text from 1950 to 2000. Your poster will allow for hands on learning to physically build a display to emphasize the relationships over and over again between context and text. In other words, your poster highlight not just on what's onscreen, but on your text's precedents and the dominant ideologies structuring discursive constructions of race, gender, or sexuality in and around your text.

Posters are a visual representation of your research. They are designed to display visual and written information on a topic in an easy to understand manner. Posters are carefully designed to make an argument about your topic. Successful posters create an effective balance between visual interest and historical explanation.

Format: Your poster will be comprised of three panels—the first should draw viewers' attention to salient aspects of your selected **text**, the second to its **historical context**, and the third to its **industrial context**. Your poster should have at least one credible source per group member on your poster. If you are in a group of five, you need at least five credible sources on the poster.

A good design should be a mix of quotation, evidence, labels, key media terms, and pictures that express your ideas clearly.

Process:

Step 1 – Pick a popular culture text case study between 1950 and 2000.

Step 2 – Research everything about your text and how it represents the social power and cultural identities of its era.

Step 3 – Make an outline for each panel of textual, historical, and industrial analysis.

Step 4 – Gather the evidence and supporting materials you will use to support your thesis and to describe the relationship between your text and the histories of race, gender, or sexuality in the United States.

Step 5 – Plan out your poster. Organization, colors, font, size, etc.

Step 6 – Avoid clutter. Everything should be there for a reason. Keep it neat. Use titles to organize information.

Step 7 – Make sure your poster is clear and easy to understand.

Step 8 – Print out and tape your works cited to the back of the poster board.

Step 9 – Proofread.

Museum Walk Worksheet

Name: _____

Directions: You will pick 1 poster from each of the three categories (Race/Ethnicity, Gender, and Sexuality) and fill out the answers below. You may NOT pick your own group's poster. Turn this worksheet in at the front of the class when you are done.

Gender Poster topic: _____

Name one specific historical component that influenced this text.

Name one way the industry shapes this text.

What was the best source and why?

What was your favorite thing you learned from this poster?

Race/Ethnicity Poster topic: _____

Name one specific historical component that influenced this text.

Name one way the industry shapes this text.

What was the best source and why?

What was your favorite thing you learned from this poster?

Sexuality Poster topic: _____

Name one specific historical component that influenced this text.

Name one way the industry shapes this text.

What was the best source and why?

What was your favorite thing you learned from this poster?

GRADING RUBRIC— UNIT 4: MUSEUM WALK EXHIBIT POSTER

	Exemplary	Proficient	Developing	Beginning
Thesis/ Central Idea 20 points	The poster explicitly and thoroughly defines the dominant ideologies of socio-historic context. (20–18 points).	The poster defines the dominant ideologies of socio-historic context. (17–16 points).	The poster defines some reasonable ideologies of socio-historic context but might be missing a larger picture. (15–14 points).	The poster begins to define some reason-able ideologies of socio-historic context but is missing the larger picture. (13–0 points).
Supporting Materials 30 points	The poster contains enough valid evidence to support its thesis and to create an effective balance between visual interest and historical explanation. (30–27 points).	There is enough valid evidence to support the poster's thesis. (26–24 points).	The poster still needs a few pieces of valid evidence to support the poster's thesis. (23–21 points).	The poster still needs much more valid evidence to support the poster's thesis. (20–0 points).
Design 30 points	The poster has a unique/ creative aspect to it that adds to its proposed thesis. It is also professional in appearance – it is neat, includes titles, effectively uses space, all text/visuals easy to see. (30–27 points).	The poster is profes-sional in appearance – it is neat, includes titles, effectively uses space, all text/visuals easy to see. (26–24 points).	Much of the poster is pro-fessional in appearance – it is still needs work in one or two of the fol-lowing: is neat, includes titles, effectively uses space, all text/visuals easy to see. (23–21 points).	The poster still needs work in several of the fol-lowing: is neat, includes titles, effectively uses space, all text/visuals easy to see. (20–0 points).
Bibliog-raphy 10 points	The bibliography con-tains at least one credible source per group member and uses a consistent and correct format – whether MLA or APA. (10–9 points).	Most of the sources in the bibliography are credible and use a con-sistent format – whether MLA or APA. (8 points).	Some of the sources in the bibliography are cred-ible. Bibliography format has some errors or does not follow a consistent format. (7 points).	Few of the bibliography sources are credible. Bibliography format has several errors and does not follow a consistent format. (6–0 points).
Mechanics 10 points	Few to no distracting errors in spelling, gram-mar, or mechanics. (10–9 points).	Some distracting errors in spelling, grammar, or mechanics. (8 points).	Several distracting errors in spelling, grammar, or mechanics. (7 points).	Too many distracting errors to be considered a final draft. (6–0 points).

FINAL ESSAY: PEER REVIEW (DRAFT – FOR *WRITER* WORKSHEET)

The following questions are to be filled out by the **Writer (you) before the Peer Review Session**
The strongest parts of my essay are:

-

-

One or two things I would appreciate your comments on are:

-

-

**Staple YOUR "Writer" and "Reviewer" Worksheets to
ONE copy of your Draft before the Workshop.
-Your "For Writer" Worksheet should go on Top.**

Note: You'll be turning in the blank copy of your Draft and taking home the marked copy.

FINAL ESSAY: PEER REVIEW (DRAFT – FOR REVIEWER WORKSHEET)

Writer's Name	
Reviewer's Name	

*These questions are to be filled out by the **reviewer of your paper.***

1. Read over answers given on the "For Writer" worksheet so that you can keep these areas in mind as you read the draft.

2. When reading over the draft, look for the following essential elements and check (✓) next to each that appears:

Introduction	Body - Structure	Body - Content	Conclusion	☐ Works Cited Page
☐ Hook	☐ Indents & Paragraphs	☐	☐ Signal end	
☐ Relate			☐ Summary/review	
☐ Thesis (Purpose)	☐ Transitions		☐ Creative close	**Paper Length (4-6 pg.s)**
☐ Point Preview	☐ Organized by Sections			☐ Too short
				☐ Appropriate length
				☐ Too long

3. As you read the draft in depth, make a **BOLD line under what you understand as the thesis statement.** Make a box around any areas that are confusing (either because of sentence structure or because they expressed concepts that were difficult to follow) and circle if you notice a grammar or formatting error.

4. Answer the following questions:

   A. What is the #1 strength of the essay?

   B. What are some other strong aspects of the essay? What really works?
      •
      •

   C. What is the #1 thing the writer should work on when revising this essay?

   D. What are some other weak aspects?
      •
      •

   F. Is the *Hook* (**and** *Relate*) relevant and appealing? Can you suggest any alternatives that would make someone *want* to read this essay?
      •
      •

   G. Quality of Source/Application (Is it academic? Does it provide insight & commentary for the medium, text, content, or method? Or, is it merely descriptive? Any suggestions for an alternate source?)
      •
      •

   H. Other suggestions ("Eyeball Test," Conclusion, Sources, Depth/Knowledge/Accuracy, Other, etc.)
      • Formatting/Organization:
      • Mechanics/Fluency:
      • Quality of Content:

5. Go over the writer's draft with her/him and explain all of your unchecked elements, squiggly lines, and circled items. Suggest ways in which a transition, clearer wording, or an additional detail would help out.

89

Name _____

GROUP PEER EVALUATION WORKSHEET

Class time: _____ **Section:** _____ **Group number:** _____

Directions: In the space below, honestly evaluate the work of ALL group members – including you – by using a scale from 0 to 30. I will then average the scores to determine each group member's grade out of 30 points.

In each category, give 0–6 points. Then, total up all those points at the bottom for their score *out of 30.*

0 = Didn't Complete	2 = Below Average	4 = Above Average	6 = Perfect
1 = Poor	3 = Average	5 = Superior	

THESE INDIVIDUAL EVALUATIONS and SCORES WILL NOT BE SEEN BY YOUR GROUP MEMBERS!

Don't base your evaluations on friendships or personality conflicts. Your input can be a valuable indicator to help assess contributions in a fair manner, based on your perceptions of how hard you worked in comparison to the other group members.

Evaluation Criteria	Group Member #1's YOUR Name: _____	Group Member #2's Name: _____	Group Member #3's Name: _____	Group Member #4's Name: _____	Group Member #5's Name: _____	Ex.: *George Costanza* _____
How well did this group member complete his/her assigned tasks for the group?						5
How would you rate the quality of this person's work?						5
How would you rate the timeliness of the work?						4
How would you rate the ease of communication with this person?						3
Overall, how would you rank this group member's attitude & performance in the group?						5 *(5+5+4+3+5=22)*
Total	_____/30	_____/30	_____/30	_____/30	_____/30	**22/30**

*If there are any notes or comments you would like to make about your group members, put them in the space below (and feel free to continue on the back of the page).

_____

_____

Name _____

POP CULTURE INVENTORY

Do you own or have access to the following technologies? *(Circle if you own it; * if you have access to it but do not own it. Also, write next to it how many hours you spend using each type of technology per week.)*

Television	Cable
Computer	Netflix
iPhone	DVD Player
Android phone	Blu-Ray Player
iPad or tablet computer	Video game system
CD Player	VCR
Cassette player	Satellite radio
Record player	Newspaper/magazine subscript.
iTunes	Other: _____
Pandora/ Spotify	

How many songs (if any) do you have on your phone? _____ **How many CDs do you own?** _____

How many movie DVDs do you own? _____ **How many television series on DVD do you own?** _____

How many books *(for pleasure)* **do you own?** _____

Please list your favorite: **Please list your** *least* **favorite:**

Band or musical artist	_____	_____
Song	_____	_____
Genre of music	_____	_____
Movie	_____	_____
Genre of movie	_____	_____
Television show	_____	_____
Book	_____	_____
Author	_____	_____
Sports team	_____	_____
Artist (painter, etc.)	_____	_____